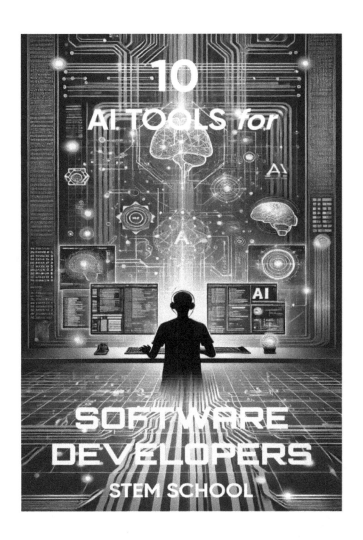

10 AI Tools Every Software Developer Must Know

Automate Coding, Debugging & Optimization

By

STEM School

This Page Left Intentionally Blank

Contents

Chapter 1

Introduction to AI in Software Development

Artificial Intelligence (AI) has revolutionized numerous industries, and software development is no exception. Over the years, AI has evolved from being a theoretical concept to a powerful tool that assists developers in coding, debugging, and optimizing software applications. The introduction of AI into software development has significantly transformed how programmers write code, detect errors, and enhance performance. This chapter provides an in-depth look into how AI is shaping the future of software development and introduces the key concepts and tools covered in this book.

The Evolution of AI in Coding and Optimization

The integration of AI into software development has progressed through several distinct phases

Early Automation (1950s–1980s) The first use of computers for coding automation dates back to the 1950s when early programming languages like FORTRAN and COBOL were introduced. These languages simplified programming tasks but still required significant manual effort.

Rule-Based Expert Systems (1990s) By the 1990s, software development had started incorporating expert systems—AI models based on predefined rules. These systems could detect simple errors and provide recommendations but lacked the ability to learn from experience.

Machine Learning and AI-Assisted Development (2000s–2010s) The rise of machine learning (ML) and natural language processing (NLP) enabled AI to analyze patterns in code, suggest improvements, and automate repetitive tasks. AI-driven debugging tools became more sophisticated, helping developers detect and resolve errors more efficiently.

Modern AI-Powered Development (2020s–Present) Today, AI-driven development tools go beyond simple automation. They provide predictive code completion, intelligent debugging, and real-time performance optimization. Advanced models such as OpenAI's Codex, DeepCode, and TabNine assist programmers in writing cleaner and more efficient code.

This evolution has led to the development of powerful AI-driven coding assistants that enhance the overall development process, significantly reducing the time and effort required to build and maintain software applications.

How AI Enhances Productivity

The impact of AI on software development is profound. It provides several benefits that streamline the development lifecycle

Enhanced Productivity AI-powered tools reduce the time developers spend writing code by offering auto-completions, suggestions, and pre-written code snippets. This allows developers to focus on higher-level problem-solving rather than spending hours writing repetitive code.

Error Reduction AI-based debugging tools analyze code in real-time, detecting potential errors, vulnerabilities, and inefficiencies. They can suggest fixes and even automatically resolve certain issues, reducing the chances of human error.

Optimized Workflows AI helps manage workflows by prioritizing tasks, suggesting best practices, and automating repetitive processes such as testing and deployment. AI-driven DevOps tools integrate with CI/CD pipelines to ensure smoother software releases.

Table 1.1 Impact of AI on Software Development

Aspect	Traditional Development	AI-Assisted Development
Coding Speed	Slower due to manual input	Faster with AI-generated suggestions
Error Detection	Requires manual debugging	AI identifies and corrects errors in real time
Workflow Management	Requires human intervention for optimization	AI automates testing, deployment, and CI/CD processes
Code	Manual code	AI optimizes performance

Aspect	Traditional Development	AI-Assisted Development
Optimization	reviews	automatically

These improvements have enabled developers to work more efficiently and deliver higher-quality software products.

Machine Learning, Natural Language Processing

To fully understand AI's role in software development, it is essential to grasp three fundamental concepts

Machine Learning (ML) This is a subset of AI that enables computers to learn patterns and make predictions based on data. ML models help software development tools understand common coding practices and suggest optimized solutions.

Natural Language Processing (NLP) NLP allows computers to understand and generate human language. In software development, NLP-powered AI can interpret natural-language queries and translate them into executable code, making coding more accessible.

Automation AI-driven automation reduces the need for manual intervention by performing repetitive tasks such as testing, deployment, and bug detection. This enables developers to focus on more creative and complex problems.

The combination of these concepts makes modern AI tools highly effective in assisting developers, leading to better efficiency and accuracy in software development.

Figure 1.1 AI in the Software Development Lifecycle

Below is a simple illustration of where AI is applied in the software development lifecycle

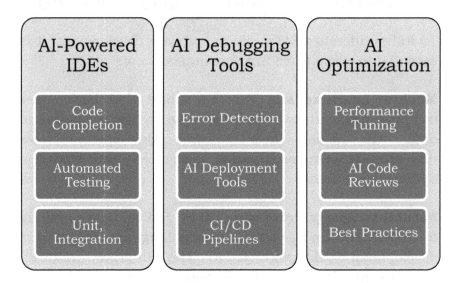

This diagram visually represents how AI plays a role at different stages of software development, from writing and debugging code to optimizing and deploying applications.

Overview of the 10 AI Tools Covered in the Book

Throughout this book, we will explore ten AI-driven tools that have been designed to assist software developers in coding, debugging, and optimizing their workflows. Each tool offers unique features that cater to different aspects of the development process. The following table provides an overview of these tools

Table 1.2 AI Tools for Software Development

Tool Name	Primary Function	Key Features
GitHub Copilot	AI-powered code completion	Predicts and suggests entire functions and snippets
DeepCode	AI-driven code analysis	Detects vulnerabilities and suggests improvements
TabNine	AI-based autocomplete	Enhances coding speed with deep learning models
Kite	Intelligent coding assistant	Context-aware code suggestions
OpenAI Codex	AI-driven programming model	Translates natural language into code
Sourcery	Automated code refactoring	Optimizes code for readability and efficiency
CodeT5	AI-powered code generation	Generates code from descriptions

Tool Name	Primary Function	Key Features
PolyCoder	Open-source AI coding model	Assists in multi-language programming
IntelliCode	AI-enhanced developer assistance	Provides smart recommendations within IDEs
Jupyter AI	AI integration for notebooks	Enhances data science and machine learning workflows

Each chapter in this book will focus on one of these tools, discussing its functionality, practical applications, and best practices for integration into your development workflow.

Artificial Intelligence is no longer just a futuristic concept in software development—it is a powerful reality that is reshaping how code is written, optimized, and deployed. AI-driven tools enhance productivity, reduce errors, and optimize workflows, making software development faster, more efficient, and less prone to human mistakes. As we progress through this book, we will explore ten of the most impactful AI tools that developers can use to improve their efficiency and code quality. By understanding the evolution, benefits, and key concepts behind AI in software development, readers will gain a solid foundation to use these cutting-edge tools effectively. The next chapter will delve deeper into the first AI tool, GitHub Copilot, and explore how it assists developers in writing high-quality code with minimal effort.

Chapter 2

AI-Powered Code Generation with GitHub Copilot

Artificial Intelligence (AI) is rapidly transforming software development, making it more efficient, intuitive, and powerful. One of the most groundbreaking AI-driven tools available today is **GitHub Copilot**, an AI-powered code assistant that accelerates development by providing real-time code suggestions, autocompleting functions, and even generating entire blocks of code based on contextual understanding. By harnessing the power of **OpenAI Codex**, Copilot understands programming syntax, logic, and best practices to assist developers in writing cleaner, more efficient code with minimal effort.

This chapter explores GitHub Copilot in depth, detailing its functionalities, underlying technology, installation process, and practical implementation. By the end, readers will gain hands-on experience using Copilot to build a simple web application, using AI-generated code to streamline development.

How GitHub Copilot Works

GitHub Copilot functions as an **AI pair programmer**, assisting developers in writing code by predicting what they need next. It operates directly within popular Integrated Development Environments (IDEs), such as **Visual Studio Code (VS Code), JetBrains IDEs, and Neovim**, making it accessible to developers across various programming languages and frameworks.

When a developer begins typing, Copilot analyzes the context of the code and suggests relevant snippets, functions, or entire blocks of logic. It can generate **boilerplate code, suggest function implementations, optimize existing code, and even provide inline documentation**. This allows developers to focus on problem-solving rather than writing repetitive or boilerplate code.

The following diagram illustrates the working mechanism of Copilot within an IDE

Figure 2.1 GitHub Copilot Workflow

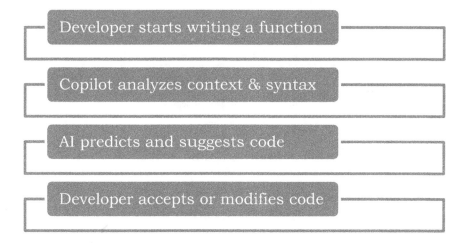

This process occurs in real-time, allowing seamless interaction between the developer and Copilot, resulting in **faster coding, fewer errors, and enhanced productivity**.

Technical Deep Dive OpenAI Codex

GitHub Copilot is powered by **OpenAI Codex**, a sophisticated AI model trained on vast amounts of publicly available code, including open-source repositories, documentation, and programming best practices. Codex is a specialized version of **GPT-3**, designed to understand and generate code in multiple programming languages, including Python, JavaScript, Java, C++, and more.

The following table outlines the technical aspects of OpenAI Codex and its role in Copilot

Table 2.1 Technical Overview of OpenAI Codex

Feature	Description
Model Type	AI-powered language model for code generation
Training Data	Open-source code, documentation, and programming tutorials
Programming Languages	Supports Python, JavaScript, C++, Java, TypeScript, and more
Context Understanding	Analyzes code structure, syntax, and intent
Deployment	Integrated with GitHub Copilot in VS

Feature	Description
	Code, JetBrains, and Neovim
Security	Implements safeguards to avoid generating insecure code

Codex operates by **understanding natural language prompts**, meaning a developer can simply type a comment describing a function, and Copilot will generate the corresponding code. For example, if a developer writes

Function to calculate the factorial of a number

Copilot might generate the following implementation

```
def factorial(n)
    if n == 0 or n == 1
        return 1
    else
        return n * factorial(n - 1)
```

This **contextual awareness and predictive capability** make Copilot an invaluable tool for both beginner and experienced developers.

Configuring GitHub Copilot in VS Code

To fully utilize GitHub Copilot, it must be properly installed and configured in an IDE. The following step-by-step guide

17

explains how to set up Copilot in **Visual Studio Code (VS Code)**

Step 1 Install VS Code

Ensure that **VS Code** is installed on your system. It can be downloaded from https //code.visualstudio.com/.

Step 2 Install the GitHub Copilot Extension

1. Open VS Code and navigate to the **Extensions Marketplace** by pressing Ctrl + Shift + X.
2. Search for **GitHub Copilot** in the search bar.
3. Click **Install** to add the extension to VS Code.

Step 3 Sign in to GitHub

After installation, GitHub Copilot requires authentication

1. Click on the **Copilot icon** in the bottom-right corner of VS Code.
2. Sign in to your **GitHub account**.
3. Ensure that your account has **GitHub Copilot enabled** (subscription required).

Step 4 Configure Copilot Settings

1. Go to **Settings** (Ctrl + , in VS Code).
2. Search for **GitHub Copilot** and adjust preferences, such as
   o Enable/disable Copilot suggestions.

- o Set keybindings for code completions.
- o Adjust privacy settings.

Once configured, Copilot will start suggesting code in real-time as you type.

Simple Web Application with Copilot's Assistance

To demonstrate the power of GitHub Copilot, we will create a **simple web application** using **HTML, CSS, and JavaScript**. The application will allow users to enter their name, and it will display a greeting message.

Step 1 Creating the Project Structure

Inside VS Code, create a new folder and add the following files

- index.html
- style.css
- script.js

Step 2 Writing the HTML File

Open index.html and type the following comment

<!-- Basic HTML structure with a text input and button -->

Copilot will generate

```
<!DOCTYPE html>
<html lang="en">
```

```
<head>
    <meta charset="UTF-8">
    <meta name="viewport" content="width=device-width, initial-
scale=1.0">
    <title>Greeting App</title>
    <link rel="stylesheet" href="style.css">
</head>
<body>
    <h1>Enter Your Name </h1>
    <input type="text" id="nameInput" placeholder="Your Name">
    <button onclick="greetUser()">Greet Me</button>
    <p id="greetingMessage"></p>
    <script src="script.js"></script>
</body>
</html>
```

Step 3 Adding Styles with CSS

In style.css, type the comment

/* Basic styling for the greeting app */

Copilot will generate

```
body {
    font-family  Arial, sans-serif;
    text-align  center;
    margin-top  50px;
}
input {
    padding  10px;
    margin  10px;
}
button {
```

```
    padding 10px;
    background-color  blue;
    color  white;
    border  none;
    cursor  pointer;
}
```

Step 4 Implementing JavaScript Logic

In script.js, type the comment

// Function to display a greeting message

Copilot will generate

```
function greetUser() {
    let name = document.getElementById("nameInput").value;
    document.getElementById("greetingMessage").innerText    =
"Hello, " + name + "!";
}
```

Step 5 Running the Web Application

Open index.html in a browser, enter a name, and click the button to see Copilot's AI-generated code in action.

GitHub Copilot represents a paradigm shift in how software is written, significantly improving efficiency by providing AI-driven code assistance. By using **OpenAI Codex**, it understands context, predicts code, and streamlines development. This chapter explored its functionalities, technical foundations, installation, and practical application in building a **simple web application**. Moving

21

forward, the next chapter will introduce **DeepCode**, an AI-powered code analysis tool that enhances software quality by detecting vulnerabilities and optimizing code performance.

Chapter 3

AI-Based Code Review with DeepCode

Software development is not just about writing code; it is equally about ensuring the quality, security, and efficiency of that code. This is where **AI-based code review tools** come into play, helping developers detect vulnerabilities, logic errors, and inefficiencies early in the development process. One of the most advanced AI-driven code review tools available today is **DeepCode**.

DeepCode acts as an **AI-powered static analysis tool** that scans source code, identifies potential issues, and suggests improvements in real time. Unlike traditional linters or syntax checkers, DeepCode employs **machine learning, pattern recognition, and static code analysis** to understand deeper logical flaws, security vulnerabilities, and performance bottlenecks.

In this chapter, we will explore how DeepCode enhances software quality through **automated code reviews**. We will examine the technology that powers it, walk through its setup and configuration, and perform a real-world project where we analyze and optimize an open-source software project using DeepCode's insights.

Understanding How DeepCode Works

DeepCode operates as an **AI-powered static analysis engine** that continuously scans source code for potential issues. It integrates with **popular version control systems such as GitHub, GitLab, and Bitbucket** to provide real-time feedback during code commits and pull requests.

Unlike traditional code review tools that rely on predefined rule sets, DeepCode uses **machine learning models trained on millions of open-source repositories** to understand common programming patterns, security vulnerabilities, and logic errors. This enables it to provide **highly accurate and context-aware recommendations** for developers.

The process of AI-based code review with DeepCode follows these stages

Figure 3.1 How DeepCode Analyzes Code

This AI-powered approach ensures that **errors are caught before deployment**, reducing the risk of software failures, security breaches, and poor performance.

AI-Powered Static Code Analysis

DeepCode uses **static code analysis** to examine source code without executing it. This approach allows it to detect **logical inconsistencies, security flaws, and inefficiencies** before they manifest as runtime errors.

To achieve this, DeepCode utilizes

Machine Learning Models Trained on billions of lines of code from public and private repositories, DeepCode can detect hidden patterns and common errors that traditional static analyzers might miss.

Syntax and Semantic Analysis DeepCode understands not only syntax rules but also the deeper semantics of code, allowing it to identify **dead code, inefficient algorithms, and potential security risks**.

AI-Powered Pattern Recognition Instead of using fixed rule sets, DeepCode continuously learns from new codebases, enabling it to detect novel programming issues dynamically.

Natural Language Processing (NLP) Helps interpret variable names, comments, and function names, improving the accuracy of recommendations.

The table below outlines the key differences between **traditional static code analyzers** and **DeepCode's AI-based approach**

Table 3.1 DeepCode vs. Traditional Code Analysis

Feature	Traditional Static Analysis	DeepCode AI-Based Analysis
Rule-Based Detection	Uses predefined rule sets	Learns from real-world codebases
False Positives	High false positive rate	Reduced false positives with contextual understanding
Security Detection	Basic vulnerability checks	Advanced security threat detection
Performance Insights	Limited recommendations	Identifies inefficient algorithms
Continuous Learning	No learning capability	AI continuously improves from new data

DeepCode's ability to **learn from real-world coding patterns** makes it significantly more effective at identifying **subtle programming mistakes and performance bottlenecks** than conventional static analyzers.

Setting Up DeepCode for Automated Code Reviews

To fully utilize DeepCode's potential, developers need to integrate it into their workflow. This section provides a step-by-step guide on setting up DeepCode for **automated code reviews in GitHub repositories**.

Step 1 Creating a GitHub Repository

Before using DeepCode, ensure you have a GitHub repository with source code that you want to analyze. If you don't have one, create a new repository at https //github.com/.

Step 2 Installing DeepCode

DeepCode offers integrations for **GitHub, GitLab, Bitbucket, and local environments**. To use it in GitHub

1. Visit DeepCode's website and sign up with a GitHub account.
2. Grant **repository access** to allow DeepCode to analyze the source code.
3. Select the repositories you want DeepCode to scan.
4. DeepCode will automatically start analyzing the codebase.

Step 3 Viewing Code Review Insights

Once DeepCode scans the repository, it presents an interactive dashboard with detected **security**

vulnerabilities, logic errors, and optimization suggestions. Developers can

- Click on **each issue** to view AI-generated recommendations.
- Accept or reject suggestions.
- Apply fixes directly from the dashboard or IDE integration.

Step 4 Automating Code Reviews in Pull Requests

DeepCode integrates into **GitHub Actions**, allowing it to scan every pull request before merging. This ensures **no buggy or insecure code** is introduced into the project.

Open-Source Project Using DeepCode

To see DeepCode's AI in action, we will analyze an **open-source Python project** for potential vulnerabilities and inefficiencies.

Step 1 Cloning the Project

For this example, we will analyze an open-source project such as **Flask**, a lightweight web framework for Python. Clone the repository using

```
git clone https //github.com/pallets/flask.git
cd flask
```

Step 2 Running DeepCode Analysis

Once the repository is connected to DeepCode, it will scan for potential issues. The AI might detect

- **Unused variables**
- **Security vulnerabilities in input handling**
- **Inefficient loops and redundant conditions**

Step 3 Reviewing and Applying Fixes

DeepCode provides recommendations such as

Example Fixing an Inefficient Loop

Before optimization

```
for i in range(len(items))
    print(items[i])
```

DeepCode suggests replacing it with a more Pythonic approach

```
for item in items
    print(item)
```

This improves **code readability and execution speed**.

Example Fixing a Security Issue

Before optimization

```
password = input("Enter password  ")
if password == "admin"
   print("Access Granted")
```

DeepCode flags this as a **hardcoded password vulnerability**, suggesting using **secure authentication methods instead**. DeepCode represents a significant advancement in **AI-powered software quality assurance**. Unlike traditional static code analyzers, it employs **machine learning, pattern recognition, and continuous learning** to detect security vulnerabilities, logic errors, and inefficiencies with high accuracy. This chapter explored DeepCode's functionalities, its **technical foundation in AI-based static analysis**, the **step-by-step process of integrating it into GitHub repositories**, and a **hands-on project demonstrating its real-world benefits**.

Chapter 4

AI-Driven Debugging with AI Bug Finder

Software development is a complex process, and one of the most time-consuming aspects of it is debugging. Identifying, diagnosing, and fixing bugs can take up a significant portion of a developer's workflow, slowing down project timelines and reducing efficiency. Traditional debugging methods rely on manually reading error logs, setting breakpoints, and using test cases to isolate faults. However, the rise of artificial intelligence (AI) has revolutionized debugging by introducing **AI-powered bug detection and automatic fix suggestions**.

Among the cutting-edge AI-driven debugging tools available today, **AI Bug Finder** stands out as an advanced system that **detects, analyzes, and suggests fixes for software bugs in real-time**. Unlike conventional debugging methods that depend on developers manually tracking down issues, AI Bug Finder uses **machine learning models trained on vast amounts of code** to identify patterns in errors and automatically recommend corrections.

This chapter explores how AI Bug Finder enhances software debugging, diving deep into the technology behind its error analysis capabilities. A **step-by-step hands-on implementation guide** will walk you through integrating AI Bug Finder into a Python project, and we will conclude with a **real-world project demonstrating how to debug and fix errors in a sample application using AI-driven insights**.

Understanding AI Bug Finder

AI Bug Finder operates as an **intelligent bug detection system** that continuously monitors code execution and flags potential errors before they cause system failures. Traditional debugging methods involve **manual code inspection, running test cases, and using print statements or breakpoints** to isolate errors. While effective, these methods are often time-intensive and require significant expertise.

In contrast, AI Bug Finder employs **deep learning models** to automatically identify errors, classify them based on severity, and provide **code-level recommendations** for fixes. The tool integrates seamlessly with modern **Integrated Development Environments (IDEs)** such as **Visual Studio Code, PyCharm, and JetBrains**, as well as with **version control platforms like GitHub and GitLab**.

The core workflow of AI Bug Finder follows a structured process, as illustrated in the diagram below

Figure 4.1 AI Bug Finder's Debugging Workflow

Through **real-time analysis and automated suggestions**, AI Bug Finder significantly accelerates debugging, reducing the need for exhaustive manual checks.

How AI Models Analyze Error Patterns

AI Bug Finder relies on a combination of **machine learning, natural language processing (NLP), and pattern recognition** to analyze source code and detect errors. Traditional debugging tools operate based on **static code analysis or runtime debugging**, but AI Bug Finder goes beyond these techniques by continuously learning from millions of software repositories, identifying common programming errors, and recommending **context-aware solutions**.

The AI-driven error analysis process consists of several key components

Code Parsing and Tokenization

When a developer writes code, AI Bug Finder **parses the source code into tokens**—small units that represent keywords, variables, functions, and operators. By converting raw code into structured data, the system can effectively analyze syntax and structure.

Error Pattern Recognition

Using a vast database of known programming bugs and best practices, AI Bug Finder **compares the scanned code with historical error patterns**. It uses **deep learning models trained on open-source repositories like GitHub, Stack Overflow, and enterprise codebases** to identify common bug signatures.

Contextual Understanding through NLP

Unlike traditional static analyzers, AI Bug Finder understands **the context of the code**. For instance, if a developer mistakenly initializes a variable incorrectly but does not use it, the tool **prioritizes this warning lower** compared to a division-by-zero error, which could lead to program crashes.

Automated Fix Generation

Once an error is detected, AI Bug Finder generates **fix suggestions** based on historical solutions from similar bug patterns. The recommendations are ranked based on their likelihood of resolving the issue with minimal side effects.

The table below compares **traditional debugging methods** with **AI-driven debugging using AI Bug Finder**

Table 4.1   Traditional Debugging vs. AI Bug Finder

Feature	Traditional Debugging	AI Bug Finder Debugging
Manual Code Inspection	Requires manual effort	AI scans and detects bugs automatically
Error Classification	Basic syntax error checks	Categorizes errors based on impact
Fix Recommendations	No automated suggestions	AI suggests optimized fixes
Time Efficiency	Slower, requires manual testing	Faster with real-time debugging
Continuous Learning	No learning mechanism	Learns from millions of codebases

By using AI-powered debugging, developers can **significantly reduce debugging time**, ensuring cleaner, error-free code faster than traditional debugging approaches.

Integrating AI Bug Finder into a Python Project

To experience AI-driven debugging firsthand, let's integrate **AI Bug Finder into a Python project** and observe how it detects and resolves errors.

Step 1 Installing AI Bug Finder Plugin

AI Bug Finder is available as an **IDE extension** for **VS Code, PyCharm, and JetBrains.** To install it

1. Open **VS Code** or **PyCharm**.
2. Navigate to **Extensions/Plugins** and search for **AI Bug Finder**.
3. Click **Install** and restart your IDE.

Step 2   Writing a Python Script with Intentional Bugs

Create a Python script (buggy_script.py) with a few common programming errors

```
def divide_numbers(a, b)
    return a / b  # Potential division by zero

numbers = [1, 2, 3, 4]
print(numbers[5])  # Index out of range
```

```
user_input = input("Enter a number  ")
print("The square is ", user_input ** 2)    # Type error   string
cannot be squared
```

Step 3 Running AI Bug Finder Analysis

When you **run the script**, AI Bug Finder immediately detects errors and provides suggested fixes.

Step 4 Applying Fixes Suggested by AI Bug Finder

The AI-generated fixes may include

Example Fixing Division by Zero

Before

```
def divide_numbers(a, b)
    return a / b
```

After AI Suggestion

```
def divide_numbers(a, b)
    return a / b if b != 0 else "Error  Division by zero"
```

Example Fixing Index Error

Before

```
print(numbers[5])
```

After AI Suggestion

```
if len(numbers) > 5
    print(numbers[5])
else
    print("Error  Index out of range")
```

By applying these AI-powered suggestions, the script becomes **more robust and error-free**.

Fixing Issues in a Sample Application

To showcase AI Bug Finder's capabilities, we will analyze and debug a **sample Flask application** with errors.

1. **Clone a buggy Flask application** from GitHub using

   ```
   git clone https //github.com/sample-flask-app.git
   cd sample-flask-app
   ```

2. **Run the AI Bug Finder analysis** in your IDE.
3. **Fix detected bugs** such as **misconfigured routes, database connection errors, and incorrect API calls**.

Through this project, you will experience **how AI can accelerate debugging**, ensuring a **stable and efficient application**. AI-driven debugging is transforming software development, making error detection and resolution faster and more efficient. AI Bug Finder uses **machine learning, pattern recognition, and automated fix recommendations** to assist developers in identifying and resolving software bugs. By integrating AI into the debugging workflow, developers can **reduce time spent on troubleshooting, enhance code reliability, and increase productivity**.

Chapter 5

AI-Powered Code Optimization with Tabnine

Software development is a continuous process of writing, debugging, and optimizing code to achieve efficiency, maintainability, and performance. Traditionally, developers rely on their experience, best practices, and manual code reviews to refine their code. However, with the rise of artificial intelligence, AI-powered tools like **Tabnine** have revolutionized code optimization by **assisting developers with intelligent autocomplete, context-aware suggestions, and efficiency recommendations**.

Tabnine is an **AI-driven code completion assistant** that enhances developer productivity by predicting entire lines of code, reducing keystrokes, and suggesting more efficient implementations. Unlike conventional autocompletion tools that rely on static keyword-based predictions, **Tabnine uses deep learning models trained on billions of lines of code** to understand coding patterns and recommend **contextually relevant, performance-optimized code snippets**.

This chapter delves into the transformative capabilities of Tabnine, explaining how it enhances **code efficiency and developer workflow**. A **technical deep dive** explores the machine learning models behind its predictive capabilities, followed by a **step-by-step guide on configuring Tabnine for Java, Python, and JavaScript**. Finally, a **hands-on project will demonstrate how Tabnine can optimize an existing codebase** to improve readability, efficiency, and execution speed.

AI-Assisted Autocomplete and Code Efficiency

Tabnine is designed to **predict and complete code** as developers type, minimizing the need for excessive manual input and repetitive typing. Unlike standard autocompletion features in IDEs, which suggest code based on predefined syntax rules, Tabnine takes code prediction to a new level by utilizing **deep learning algorithms trained on real-world software repositories**.

At its core, Tabnine operates as an **AI-powered predictive engine** that seamlessly integrates with popular IDEs, including **Visual Studio Code, JetBrains, PyCharm, IntelliJ IDEA, and Sublime Text**. Its real-time **context-aware recommendations** help developers

Reduce repetitive coding tasks By predicting entire function bodies and code blocks, developers save time on frequently written patterns.

Enhance efficiency The AI engine learns individual coding habits, refining predictions based on user-specific styles.

Optimize performance Tabnine suggests **more efficient algorithms and coding structures**, reducing redundancy and improving execution speed.

The following diagram illustrates how **Tabnine assists developers** in writing code efficiently

Figure 5.1 Workflow of Tabnine in Code

With its **real-time suggestions**, Tabnine significantly speeds up development while **encouraging best coding practices and improving software maintainability**.

How Tabnine Learns from User Coding Patterns

Tabnine's AI-driven prediction capabilities are powered by **deep learning models trained on vast datasets** of open-source and proprietary codebases. Unlike basic autocompletion tools, which rely on syntax-based matching, Tabnine employs **Transformer-based neural networks** that enable it to understand **complex coding structures, context, and developer-specific patterns**.

The AI behind Tabnine functions through the following key mechanisms

Code Tokenization and Context Analysis

When a developer types in an IDE, Tabnine **tokenizes the input**—breaking down the code into meaningful components such as keywords, variables, and functions. Using **natural language processing (NLP),** it analyzes these tokens to determine the intended structure and predict relevant code completions.

Machine Learning-Based Prediction Model

Tabnine uses **GPT-like deep learning models** that are pre-trained on vast amounts of source code from repositories such as GitHub, Bitbucket, and GitLab. The AI model recognizes **patterns, common coding structures, and best practices** to generate optimal suggestions for developers.

Personalized Learning for User-Specific Optimization

Unlike traditional autocompletion tools, Tabnine **learns from an individual developer's coding habits over time**. It adapts to user preferences, optimizing suggestions to align with personal programming styles and frequently used functions.

AI-Driven Code Optimization

Beyond prediction, Tabnine also **recommends improvements** in **code efficiency, execution speed, and structure**. It identifies areas where loops can be optimized, conditions can be simplified, or redundant operations can be removed.

The following table highlights the **differences between standard autocompletion tools and Tabnine's AI-powered predictions**

Table 5.1 Autocomplete vs. AI-Powered Tabnine

Feature	Standard Autocomplete	Tabnine AI Prediction
Completion Method	Keyword-based	Context-aware deep learning
Learning Capability	Static, no learning	Adaptive, improves over time
Code Optimization	No efficiency checks	Suggests better performance solutions
Personalized Suggestions	Generic suggestions	Tailored to user's coding habits
Efficiency Impact	Minimal improvement	Reduces redundant code and improves speed

Tabnine's **intelligent pattern recognition and predictive capabilities** make it a **powerful assistant for developers**, ensuring not only **faster code writing** but also **more optimized and error-free implementations**.

Configuring Tabnine for Java and JavaScript

To experience **Tabnine's AI-powered code completion**, we will configure it for three popular programming languages **Java, Python, and JavaScript**.

Step 1   Installing Tabnine in Visual Studio Code

1. Open **VS Code** and navigate to **Extensions**.
2. Search for **Tabnine** and click **Install**.
3. Restart the editor for changes to take effect.

Step 2   Enabling Tabnine for Java, Python, and JavaScript

1. Open your **settings.json** file in VS Code.
2. Add the following configurations to enable Tabnine support

```
{
    "editor.inlineSuggest.enabled"  true,
    "tabnine.experimentalAutoImport"  true
}
```

3. Save and restart the editor.

Project Optimizing Codebase with Tabnine

To see **Tabnine's AI-powered code optimization in action**, let's optimize an existing Python codebase.

Original Code Unoptimized Python Sorting Function

```
def sort_numbers(arr)
    for i in range(len(arr))
        for j in range(i + 1, len(arr))
            if arr[i] > arr[j]
                arr[i], arr[j] = arr[j], arr[i]
    return arr
```

AI-Suggested Optimized Code

```
def sort_numbers(arr)
    return sorted(arr)
```

Instead of using a **nested loop for sorting**, Tabnine suggests using Python's built-in **sorted() function**, which is significantly faster and more efficient.

Optimization in JavaScript

Original Code

```
function getUserData(users) {
    let userList = [];
```

```
    for (let i = 0; i < users.length; i++) {
        userList.push(users[i].name);
    }
    return userList;
}
```

Optimized Code (Suggested by Tabnine)

```
function getUserData(users) {
    return users.map(user => user.name);
}
```

By using **map()**, Tabnine helps reduce **loop complexity** and improves **readability**. Tabnine is **revolutionizing code efficiency** by providing **AI-powered autocompletion and optimization**. Unlike traditional autocomplete tools, **Tabnine learns from individual developer patterns, offers personalized suggestions, and improves code performance**. The integration of AI in coding workflows ensures **faster development cycles, reduced redundancy, and optimized execution**.

Chapter 6

Automated Testing with Diffblue Cover

Software testing is an essential phase in the development lifecycle, ensuring that applications function as intended, remain free of critical defects, and maintain reliability over time. Traditionally, unit testing—one of the most fundamental testing techniques—requires developers to manually write test cases, which can be time-consuming and prone to human oversight. However, the integration of artificial intelligence into software development has introduced **AI-driven automated testing tools like Diffblue Cover**, which revolutionizes the way unit tests are created and executed.

Diffblue Cover is an AI-powered tool specifically designed to automatically generate unit tests for Java applications. It eliminates the need for developers to manually write extensive test cases by **analyzing the application code and producing test scripts that assess functionality, edge cases, and potential failures**. This not only accelerates the testing process but also significantly improves code coverage, ensuring that all possible scenarios are examined.

This chapter explores **how Diffblue Cover enhances software reliability, the underlying AI techniques it employs, and a step-by-step implementation guide**. Finally, we will conduct a **hands-on project where Diffblue Cover will be used to generate unit tests for a Java application**, demonstrating its real-world applicability.

AI-Generated Unit Tests for Java Code

Traditional unit testing requires developers to manually write test cases for each function or method in a software program. This is both tedious and error-prone, often leading to inadequate test coverage. **Diffblue Cover automates this process by using AI to generate unit tests**, significantly reducing the effort required while ensuring that **tests cover multiple execution paths, including edge cases and failure conditions**.

Diffblue Cover's functionality is based on **code analysis and test synthesis**. It examines the Java code, understands its logic, and produces unit tests with **assertions that validate expected outputs**. It seamlessly integrates with Java-based projects and works with popular testing frameworks such as **JUnit**.

The workflow of Diffblue Cover can be illustrated as follows

Figure 6.1 How Diffblue Cover Generates AI Unit Tests

AI-Generated Test Cases and Assertion Predictions

Diffblue Cover uses **machine learning and symbolic execution techniques** to create unit tests that maximize code coverage and identify functional defects. Its AI models analyze the **control flow, dependencies, and potential execution paths** of a Java program, ensuring that all critical functionalities are tested.

The process follows these core steps

Code Structure Analysis

Diffblue Cover **parses Java classes and methods**, identifying **input parameters, return types, and**

dependencies. This allows the AI to understand how data flows through the program.

Path Exploration with Symbolic Execution

Symbolic execution is a technique where Diffblue Cover **explores all potential execution paths** in a program. It evaluates **if-else conditions, loops, and recursive functions** to identify different ways the code can behave under various inputs.

Test Case Synthesis

Once the code structure is analyzed, Diffblue Cover **automatically generates test cases** that ensure comprehensive coverage. Each test case includes

Input values Generated dynamically based on function signatures.

Expected outputs Derived using AI models to predict correct results.

Assertions Validations that check if the function behaves as expected.

Execution and Refinement

After generating test cases, Diffblue Cover **executes them automatically**. If failures occur, it provides insights into potential issues, allowing developers to refine the code and improve reliability.

The following table compares **manual unit testing vs. AI-generated testing with Diffblue Cover**

Table 6.1 Manual Unit Testing vs. AI-Powered Testing with Diffblue Cover

Feature	Manual Unit Testing	Diffblue Cover (AI-Generated)
Test Creation Time	Slow, manual effort	Instant, AI-generated
Test Coverage	Limited by human input	Comprehensive, AI explores all paths
Error Detection	Prone to missing cases	Identifies edge cases and vulnerabilities
Maintenance	Requires manual updates	Auto-adapts to code changes

Running Diffblue Cover to Generate Tests

To implement **Diffblue Cover** in a Java project, follow these steps

Step 1 Install Diffblue Cover

1. Open **IntelliJ IDEA** and navigate to **Plugins**.
2. Search for **Diffblue Cover** and click **Install**.

3. Restart IntelliJ IDEA for the changes to take effect.

Step 2 Generate Unit Tests

1. Open an existing Java project in IntelliJ IDEA.
2. Right-click on the class you want to test and select **"Create Tests with Diffblue Cover"**.
3. Diffblue Cover will analyze the code and generate a complete set of **JUnit test cases**.

Project   Developing an Application and Using AI-Generated Tests for Reliability

To illustrate **Diffblue Cover in action**, we will create a simple Java **Bank Account Management System** and use AI to generate unit tests.

Step 1 Create a Java Class

```java
public class BankAccount {
    private double balance;

    public BankAccount(double initialBalance) {
        this.balance = initialBalance;
    }

    public void deposit(double amount) {
        if (amount > 0) {
            balance += amount;
        }
    }
}
```

```java
    public boolean withdraw(double amount) {
        if (amount > 0 && amount <= balance) {
            balance -= amount;
            return true;
        }
        return false;
    }

    public double getBalance() {
        return balance;
    }
}
```

Step 2 Use Diffblue Cover to Generate Tests

After running Diffblue Cover, the following AI-generated test cases are produced

```java
import static org.junit.jupiter.api.Assertions.*;
import org.junit.jupiter.api.Test;

public class BankAccountTest {

    @Test
    public void testDeposit() {
        BankAccount account = new BankAccount(100);
        account.deposit(50);
        assertEquals(150, account.getBalance());
    }

    @Test
    public void testWithdraw() {
        BankAccount account = new BankAccount(100);
```

```
    assertTrue(account.withdraw(50));
    assertEquals(50, account.getBalance());
  }

  @Test
  public void testWithdrawFailure() {
    BankAccount account = new BankAccount(100);
    assertFalse(account.withdraw(200));
    assertEquals(100, account.getBalance());
  }
}
```

Step 3 Execute Tests

1. Run the **JUnit test suite**.
2. Verify that all test cases pass, ensuring that the **BankAccount class behaves correctly**.

With **Diffblue Cover, we have successfully generated unit tests in seconds**, significantly improving development efficiency and ensuring our Java application is **robust and bug-free**. AI-powered testing tools like **Diffblue Cover** have transformed the way developers ensure software reliability. By automatically generating unit tests, **Diffblue Cover reduces manual effort, increases test coverage, and enhances error detection**, leading to **more secure and stable applications**.

Chapter 7

AI-Powered Code Documentation with Mintlify

Documentation is one of the most critical aspects of software development, serving as a bridge between developers, users, and future maintainers of a project. Well-written documentation ensures that code is **understandable, maintainable, and scalable**. However, writing and maintaining documentation manually is often a tedious and time-consuming process. Many developers prioritize writing functional code over documenting it, which results in incomplete or outdated documentation that can hinder future development.

With the advancements in **Artificial Intelligence (AI) and Natural Language Processing (NLP)**, AI-powered documentation tools like **Mintlify** have emerged to **automate the process of generating, updating, and structuring documentation** for complex codebases. Mintlify utilizes AI models to **analyze code, extract meaningful explanations, and format them into clear and structured documentation**. This chapter explores how **Mintlify automates documentation generation, the technical foundations of its NLP-based approach, step-by-step implementation**, and a **real-world project where Mintlify is used to document an open-source library**.

Automating Documentation for Codebases

Mintlify is an AI-powered tool designed to **automatically generate documentation** by analyzing source code, function definitions, variables, and class structures. It extracts contextual information and **produces well-**

structured documentation with descriptions, code examples, and usage guidelines.

Unlike traditional documentation methods that rely on manual writing and upkeep, Mintlify ensures that documentation **remains up-to-date** by dynamically generating content that aligns with code modifications. This significantly reduces developer workload while improving the overall quality and accessibility of documentation.

The workflow of Mintlify can be illustrated as follows

Figure 7.1 How Mintlify Generates Documentation

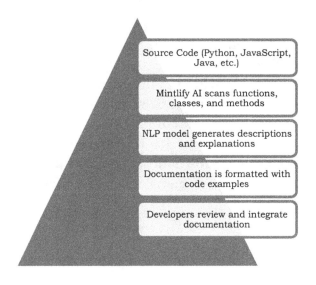

Mintlify supports **multiple programming languages**, including **Python, JavaScript, TypeScript, Go, and Java**, making it a versatile choice for documenting diverse software projects.

NLP-Based Documentation Generation

At its core, Mintlify uses **Natural Language Processing (NLP) and Machine Learning (ML) models** to analyze and extract meaningful information from source code. The key components of its AI-driven documentation generation process include **code parsing, entity recognition, context understanding, and structured formatting**.

Code Parsing and Entity Recognition

Mintlify scans the source code to identify key elements, such as **function definitions, class structures, method parameters, and return types**. It understands variable names, data types, and dependencies within the codebase.

Context Understanding with NLP

Using advanced NLP techniques, Mintlify determines the **purpose and functionality of each function or class**. It generates **natural language descriptions** that summarize what the code does, including explanations of input parameters and expected outputs.

Auto-Generation of Documentation

Once the code is analyzed, Mintlify generates **structured documentation** that includes

- **Function descriptions** Explains the purpose and role of the function.
- **Parameter details** Specifies expected inputs and data types.
- **Return values** Describes expected outputs and exceptions.
- **Code examples** Provides usage examples to demonstrate how the function works.

Continuous Documentation Updates

Mintlify integrates with **GitHub repositories** and continuously updates documentation whenever changes are made to the source code. This ensures that documentation remains **synchronized** with the latest developments.

The following table compares **traditional manual documentation vs. AI-powered documentation with Mintlify**

Table 7.1 Manual vs. AI-Powered Documentation

Feature	Manual Documentation	Mintlify (AI-Generated)
Time Required	High, manual effort	Low, automated generation
Consistency	Prone to inconsistencies	Consistently updates with code changes
Detail Level	Varies by	Comprehensive, AI

Feature	Manual Documentation	Mintlify (AI-Generated)
	developer input	ensures all functions are documented
Maintenance	Requires frequent updates	Auto-updates with code modifications

Mintlify to Document a Software Project

Mintlify provides an easy-to-use CLI and integrates seamlessly with **GitHub repositories, local projects, and CI/CD pipelines**. To implement Mintlify in a software project, follow the step-by-step guide below.

Step 1 Install Mintlify

Mintlify can be installed using **npm**. Run the following command

npm install -g @mintlify/cli

Step 2 Initialize Mintlify in Your Project

Navigate to the root directory of your project and initialize Mintlify

mintlify init

This command will scan the project and create an initial documentation structure.

Step 3 Generate Documentation

Run the following command to let Mintlify analyze the code and produce AI-generated documentation

mintlify generate

Step 4 Preview Documentation

Mintlify provides a preview feature to review the generated documentation before publishing it

mintlify preview

This allows developers to make adjustments before deploying the documentation.

Step 5 Deploy Documentation to GitHub Pages or Other Platforms

Once satisfied, deploy the documentation to a hosting platform

mintlify deploy

Mintlify supports deployment to **GitHub Pages, Netlify, and Vercel**, making it easy to publish structured and well-formatted documentation.

Project Automating Documentation for an Open-Source Library

To demonstrate Mintlify's capabilities, we will document an **open-source Python library** that provides **mathematical utilities**.

Step 1 Create a Sample Python Library

```python
class MathUtils
    """A collection of mathematical utility functions."""

    def add(self, a  float, b  float) -> float
        """Returns the sum of two numbers."""
        return a + b

    def subtract(self, a  float, b  float) -> float
        """Returns the difference between two numbers."""
        return a - b

    def multiply(self, a  float, b  float) -> float
        """Returns the product of two numbers."""
        return a * b
```

Step 2 Generate Documentation with Mintlify

Running mintlify generate on this library produces the following documentation

MathUtils

A collection of mathematical utility functions.

`add(a float, b float) -> float`
**Description **
Returns the sum of two numbers.

**Parameters **
- `a (float)` The first number.
- `b (float)` The second number.

**Returns **
- `float` The sum of `a` and `b`.

`subtract(a float, b float) -> float`
**Description **
Returns the difference between two numbers.

`multiply(a float, b float) -> float`
**Description **
Returns the product of two numbers.

This automatically generated documentation **saves time, improves clarity, and ensures consistency**. AI-powered documentation tools like **Mintlify** revolutionize how developers create, maintain, and publish software documentation. By using **NLP and AI-driven automation**, Mintlify **eliminates the burden of manual documentation**, ensures **comprehensive and up-to-date content**, and improves the overall **developer experience**.

Chapter 8

AI-Assisted DevOps with KubeSphere and DevOps AI

In the fast-evolving world of software development, DevOps has become a critical practice that bridges the gap between development and IT operations. It enables organizations to build, test, and deploy software faster and more reliably. However, traditional DevOps workflows often face challenges such as **manual configuration errors, inefficient monitoring, slow deployments, and infrastructure scaling issues**.

The integration of **Artificial Intelligence (AI) into DevOps, often called "AIOps"**, is transforming the landscape by automating **continuous integration, continuous deployment (CI/CD), infrastructure monitoring, predictive analytics, and resource scaling**. AI-assisted DevOps tools like **KubeSphere and DevOps AI** use machine learning algorithms to detect anomalies, predict system failures, optimize infrastructure usage, and enhance the efficiency of CI/CD pipelines.

This chapter explores how **AI automates DevOps tasks**, the **technical workings of AI-driven DevOps monitoring and analytics**, and a **step-by-step implementation of deploying a cloud application using AI-powered DevOps tools**. Additionally, we will build a real-world **AI-monitored deployment pipeline for a microservices application**.

Automating CI/CD and Infrastructure Monitoring

AI-assisted DevOps introduces automation at multiple levels, ensuring **faster deployments, self-healing**

infrastructure, and predictive maintenance. KubeSphere and DevOps AI enable organizations to **reduce human intervention in monitoring, automate testing, and optimize resource allocation**.

The core benefits of AI in DevOps include

Automated CI/CD Pipelines   AI optimizes continuous integration and deployment by detecting build failures, suggesting fixes, and automating rollback mechanisms.

Predictive Analytics   Machine learning models analyze system logs, network traffic, and historical data to predict failures before they occur.

Anomaly Detection and Self-Healing   AI-powered monitoring tools detect unusual behavior in the infrastructure and automatically take corrective actions.

Dynamic Resource Scaling   AI-driven auto-scaling ensures efficient resource allocation based on traffic patterns and workload demands.

Intelligent Log Analysis   AI tools process large volumes of log data in real-time to identify patterns, errors, and potential vulnerabilities.

DevOps Monitoring and Scaling

AI-Based DevOps Monitoring

Traditional DevOps monitoring relies on static thresholds and reactive incident response. AI-powered monitoring, on the other hand, uses **machine learning models to analyze real-time metrics, logs, and system behavior**.

KubeSphere integrates with **Prometheus, Elasticsearch, and Grafana** to provide real-time AI-driven insights into system performance. It can

Analyze system logs to detect irregularities in application behavior.

Identify patterns in CPU, memory, and network usage.

Trigger automated responses when anomalies are detected.

Predictive Analytics for Failure Prevention

DevOps AI platforms use predictive analytics to **forecast potential system failures** before they happen. AI models trained on **historical data and system metrics** can predict

- **Downtime risks** based on past failures.
- **Performance degradation trends** due to increasing traffic loads.
- **Security threats** by identifying unusual access patterns.

AI-Driven Auto-Scaling

In traditional DevOps, **horizontal and vertical scaling** is often manually configured. AI-powered auto-scaling **dynamically adjusts resources based on real-time demand**.

For example, an e-commerce website might experience **high traffic spikes during a sale event**. Instead of **manually provisioning extra servers**, AI-driven auto-scaling detects the demand and automatically **adds or removes computing instances**.

The following table compares **traditional DevOps monitoring vs. AI-driven DevOps**

Table 8.1 Traditional vs. AI-Assisted DevOps Monitoring

Feature	Traditional DevOps Monitoring	AI-Assisted DevOps Monitoring
Failure Detection	Based on fixed thresholds	Predictive anomaly detection
Response Mechanism	Manual intervention required	Automated, self-healing responses
Log Analysis	Requires manual inspection	AI-driven real-time insights

Feature	Traditional DevOps Monitoring	AI-Assisted DevOps Monitoring
Infrastructure Scaling	Pre-configured scaling rules	AI-driven dynamic auto-scaling

Deploying a Cloud Application with DevOps Tools

To demonstrate AI-assisted DevOps, we will **deploy a cloud-based microservices application** using KubeSphere and DevOps AI.

Step 1 Install KubeSphere on a Kubernetes Cluster

KubeSphere provides a UI-based DevOps platform that integrates with Kubernetes. To install KubeSphere, run the following command on your Kubernetes cluster

```
curl -fsSL https //raw.githubusercontent.com/kubesphere/ks-installer/master/scripts/install.sh | bash
```

After installation, access the KubeSphere dashboard at

```
http //<cluster-ip> 30880
```

Step 2 Set Up an AI-Powered CI/CD Pipeline

Using KubeSphere's DevOps module, create a **Jenkins-powered CI/CD pipeline** with AI-based monitoring.

1. **Create a new DevOps project** in the KubeSphere dashboard.
2. **Add a pipeline** using Jenkins with AI-driven anomaly detection.
3. **Integrate GitHub** for source code repository automation.
4. **Enable AI-based test automation** to detect failures before deployment.

Step 3   Configure AI-Based Monitoring with Prometheus & Grafana

To enable AI-powered monitoring, integrate **Prometheus and Grafana** with KubeSphere

```
kubectl apply -f https //raw.githubusercontent.com/prometheus-operator/kube-prometheus/main/manifests/setup/
kubectl apply -f https //raw.githubusercontent.com/prometheus-operator/kube-prometheus/main/manifests/
```

Step 4 Deploy a Microservices Application

Deploy a sample **e-commerce microservices app** using Kubernetes and KubeSphere

```
kubectl apply -f microservices-deployment.yaml
```

This will deploy a **multi-container application** monitored by AI-based DevOps tools.

AI-Monitored Deployment Pipeline

For the project, we will deploy a **real-world microservices-based e-commerce application** that includes

- **User Authentication Service**
- **Product Catalog Service**
- **Order Processing Service**

Step 1 Define Microservices in Kubernetes

```
apiVersion  apps/v1
kind  Deployment
metadata
  name  auth-service
spec
  replicas  3
  selector
    matchLabels
      app  auth-service
  template
    metadata
      labels
        app  auth-service
    spec
      containers
      - name  auth-service
        image  auth-service latest
```

Step 2   Automate   Monitoring   with KubeSphere

Use **AI-powered monitoring dashboards** to track **CPU, memory, and network usage** in real-time.

Step 3 Enable Auto-Scaling

kubectl autoscale deployment auth-service --cpu-percent=50 --min=2 --max=10

This **AI-driven auto-scaler** dynamically adjusts the number of pods based on traffic.

AI-assisted DevOps with tools like **KubeSphere and DevOps AI** enables **fully automated software deployment, predictive failure prevention, and intelligent infrastructure scaling**. By using **AI for monitoring, CI/CD automation, and resource management**, DevOps teams can **reduce downtime, improve efficiency, and ensure high system availability**.

Chapter 9

AI-Powered API Development with Postman AI

In modern software development, **Application Programming Interfaces (APIs)** play a crucial role in enabling communication between different software applications, services, and systems. APIs allow seamless interaction between web services, mobile applications, databases, and cloud platforms. However, API development involves several complex tasks, including **writing documentation, generating test cases, debugging response errors, and optimizing request performance**.

With the rise of **AI-powered development tools**, Postman AI has emerged as a leading solution for automating API-related workflows. It provides developers with **intelligent API documentation generation, automated request validation, test case recommendations, and performance optimization insights**. By using **machine learning and natural language processing (NLP), Postman AI** significantly enhances the efficiency of API development, testing, and monitoring.

This chapter explores how **Postman AI automates API workflows, the technical mechanics of AI-driven API request generation and response analysis, a step-by-step guide to implementing AI-driven API testing**, and a **real-world project demonstrating how to build and optimize an AI-powered API testing pipeline**.

Automating Documentation and Optimization

The traditional API development process requires **manual documentation, repetitive test case writing, debugging request-response errors, and manually optimizing performance**. These tasks are time-consuming and error-prone. AI-powered tools like Postman AI simplify these processes by **automating documentation, generating smart test cases, detecting anomalies in API responses, and recommending performance enhancements**.

The key capabilities of Postman AI include

Automated API Documentation AI extracts endpoint details from API definitions and automatically generates human-readable documentation.

Smart API Test Generation Postman AI suggests test cases based on API request patterns, response validation logic, and common failure scenarios.

AI-Powered Response Analysis Machine learning algorithms analyze API responses to detect inconsistencies, slow performance, and potential security vulnerabilities.

Optimized API Performance Testing AI tools measure API response times, recommend caching strategies, and identify request bottlenecks.

The following diagram illustrates the AI-powered API development workflow

Figure 9.1   AI-Powered API Development Workflow

AI-Driven API Request Generation

AI-Based API Documentation

Traditional API documentation requires **manual writing of request endpoints, parameters, headers, and response formats**, which is often tedious and prone to errors. Postman AI automates this process using **Natural Language Processing (NLP) and machine learning**. It extracts **request-response structures** from API definitions (Swagger, OpenAPI, GraphQL schemas) and converts them into **well-structured, human-readable documentation**.

AI-Powered Request Validation

Postman AI **automatically generates API test cases** by analyzing API contracts, expected inputs, and potential edge cases. AI-powered test case recommendations help developers validate

- **Input validation errors** (e.g., missing required parameters).
- **Response structure verification** (e.g., JSON schema validation).
- **Performance metrics** (e.g., response latency tracking).

AI-Driven Response Analysis and Debugging

AI models **analyze API responses** by detecting **unexpected status codes, incorrect data formats, and latency issues**. It provides **real-time debugging suggestions** to improve API reliability.

Performance Optimization Using AI

Postman AI **monitors API performance trends** and suggests improvements such as **query optimizations, load balancing techniques, and caching recommendations** to improve API response times.

The following table compares **traditional vs. AI-assisted API development**

Table 9.1 Traditional API Development vs. AI-Assisted API Development

Feature	Traditional API Development	AI-Assisted API Development
API Documentation	Manually written	AI-generated documentation
Test Case Creation	Manual test writing	AI-driven test recommendations
Request Validation	Manual debugging	AI-based validation
Response Analysis	Manual log inspection	AI-powered anomaly detection
Performance Testing	Manual profiling	AI-driven optimization suggestions

Using Postman AI to Generate Test Cases for APIs

To demonstrate **AI-driven API testing**, we will use **Postman AI** to **automate test generation and optimize API performance**.

Step 1 Install Postman and Set Up an API Collection

Postman provides a user-friendly UI for testing APIs. Download and install Postman from

https //www.postman.com/downloads/

Once installed, create a **new collection** and add an API endpoint.

Step 2 Enable AI-Powered Testing in Postman

Postman AI automatically suggests test cases. To enable this feature

1. Open Postman and navigate to **"Tests"**.
2. Click **"Generate AI-Powered Tests"** to let Postman AI create intelligent test cases.
3. Review and run AI-generated test cases against the API.

Step 3 Analyze API Response with Postman AI

Postman AI provides **real-time response analysis** by highlighting slow response times, incorrect data formats, and status code mismatches.

Step 4 Optimize API Performance Using AI Insights

Use **AI-powered recommendations** from Postman to improve request efficiency, reduce redundant queries, and cache frequently accessed responses.

Project Building and Optimizing an AI-Driven API Testing Pipeline

For this project, we will create a **fully automated API testing pipeline** using Postman AI. This pipeline will

1. **Generate AI-powered API documentation.**
2. **Automatically create API test cases.**
3. **Analyze API responses for anomalies.**
4. **Optimize API performance using AI-driven suggestions.**

Step 1 Define API Endpoints

We will test a **user authentication API** with the following endpoints

Endpoint	Method	Description
/register	POST	Registers a new user.
/login	POST	Authenticates a user.
/profile	GET	Retrieves user details.

Step 2 Generate AI-Powered API Tests

In Postman, click "**Generate AI Tests**" for each API request. Postman AI will create test cases such as

- Checking if the /login endpoint returns a 200 OK status.
- Validating that /profile returns the correct JSON structure.
- Measuring response times to detect slow requests.

Step 3 Implement AI-Driven Optimization

Using AI-powered analysis, Postman will suggest

- **Adding caching for repetitive API requests.**
- **Reducing redundant database queries to improve response time.**
- **Load balancing API requests to avoid bottlenecks.**

Step 4 Automate API Testing in CI/CD

Integrate Postman AI tests into a CI/CD pipeline using

newman run collection.json -r cli,html

This command **automates AI-generated tests**, ensuring API reliability in production.

AI-powered API development with Postman AI transforms **how APIs are documented, tested, and optimized**. By using **machine learning algorithms for request validation, test case generation, response analysis, and**

performance optimization, developers can **significantly reduce manual effort, enhance API reliability, and improve overall performance**.

Chapter 10

AI-Based Code Refactoring with Refact.ai

Code refactoring is the process of **restructuring existing code without changing its external behavior**. This practice enhances code readability, improves maintainability, and optimizes performance. However, manual refactoring can be time-consuming, error-prone, and challenging—especially when dealing with **large codebases, legacy systems, and complex dependencies**.

With the advancement of **Artificial Intelligence (AI) in software development**, AI-powered tools such as **Refact.ai** automate the refactoring process. Refact.ai analyzes code structures, identifies inefficiencies, and suggests refactoring techniques to **reduce redundancy, improve performance, and make the codebase more maintainable**.

In this chapter, we will explore how **Refact.ai automates code refactoring, the underlying AI techniques it uses to analyze code complexity, a step-by-step implementation guide**, and a **real-world project demonstrating AI-powered code optimization**.

How AI Enhances Code Refactoring

Traditional code refactoring requires **human intervention to detect code smells, redundant logic, and inefficiencies**. Developers often rely on **manual reviews and static analysis tools** to improve code quality. However, AI-based refactoring tools like Refact.ai offer a more **intelligent, automated, and scalable approach**.

Refact.ai uses **machine learning models trained on millions of code samples** to

Identify repetitive code patterns and suggest modular structures to improve maintainability.

Analyze function complexity and recommend splitting overly large methods into smaller, reusable functions.

Detect inefficient loops, redundant conditions, and unused variables to optimize performance.

Automatically rename variables and functions for better readability.

Propose design pattern implementations to enhance software architecture.

The following diagram illustrates the AI-powered code refactoring workflow

Figure 10.1 AI-Driven Code Refactoring Process

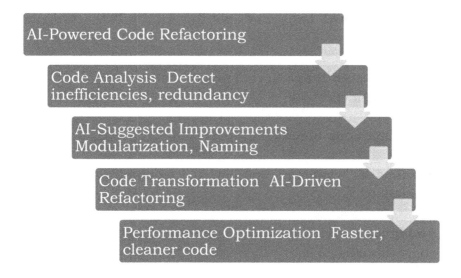

How AI Understands Code Complexity

AI-Powered Code Analysis

Refact.ai uses **Natural Language Processing (NLP) and Machine Learning (ML)** models to analyze code structure. It scans codebases for **patterns of inefficiency, duplication, and poor readability**.

The tool uses **Abstract Syntax Tree (AST) representations** to **break down code into structured elements,** allowing AI to understand the logical flow of functions, loops, and variable assignments.

AI-Driven Refactoring Recommendations

Refact.ai **detects code smells** such as

Long functions (suggests splitting into smaller, modular functions).

Deeply nested loops (recommends restructuring for clarity and efficiency).

Duplicate code blocks (suggests function abstraction).

Hardcoded values (proposes parameterization for reusability).

Ambiguous variable names (provides meaningful naming suggestions).

Code Transformation Using AI

Once AI identifies improvements, it **automatically applies refactoring techniques** such as

- **Extracting methods to eliminate redundancy.**
- **Reorganizing classes for better object-oriented design.**
- **Replacing inefficient loops with optimized alternatives.**
- **Suggesting efficient data structures for performance gains.**

The following table compares **traditional vs. AI-powered refactoring**

Table 10.1   Traditional vs. AI-Assisted Code Refactoring

Feature	Traditional Code Refactoring	AI-Assisted Code Refactoring
Code Review Process	Manual and time-consuming	AI-driven automation
Detection of Code Smells	Based on developer experience	AI-powered analysis
Refactoring Suggestions	Requires deep technical knowledge	AI-recommended improvements
Optimization Techniques	Manually implemented	AI-automated code transformation

Using Refact.ai to Refactor a Legacy Codebase

To demonstrate **AI-powered code refactoring**, we will use **Refact.ai** to optimize a **legacy Python codebase**.

Step 1 Install and Configure Refact.ai

Refact.ai can be integrated into popular code editors like **VS Code and JetBrains IDEs**. To install Refact.ai in VS Code

1. Open **VS Code** and navigate to the **Extensions Marketplace**.

93

2. Search for **"Refact.ai"** and click **"Install"**.
3. Once installed, launch the **Refact.ai panel** and connect it to your project directory.

Step 2 Analyze the Legacy Codebase

For this example, consider the following **legacy Python script** that processes customer orders

```
def process_orders(orders)
    total = 0
    for i in range(len(orders))
        total += orders[i]['amount']
    print("Total amount ", total)
    return total
```

Using Refact.ai, click **"Analyze Code"** to detect inefficiencies.

Step 3 Apply AI-Driven Refactoring

Refact.ai suggests

- **Replacing the manual loop with Python's built-in sum() function**.
- **Renaming ambiguous variables for clarity**.
- **Using type hints for better code readability**.

Refact.ai refactors the code as

```
from typing import List, Dict

def calculate_total_amount(orders  List[Dict[str, float]]) -> float
```

```
total_amount = sum(order['amount'] for order in orders)
print("Total amount ", total_amount)
return total_amount
```

Step 4 Review and Apply Suggested Changes

Once AI applies the changes, review the refactored code and test its functionality to ensure correctness.

Project Improving the Efficiency and Readability of a Large Code Project Using AI

For this project, we will use **Refact.ai to refactor a large codebase**. The objective is to

1. **Identify redundant code and replace it with reusable functions.**
2. **Optimize inefficient loops and data structures.**
3. **Improve variable and function naming for readability.**
4. **Enhance performance by replacing outdated logic with AI-suggested improvements.**

Step 1 Load a Complex Codebase

Consider a **large e-commerce application** with functions for order processing, customer management, and payment handling.

Component	Code Complexity Issue
Order Processing	Redundant loops, hardcoded values
Customer Database	Inefficient SQL queries
Payment Gateway	Overly complex functions

Step 2 Run Refact.ai Analysis

Execute Refact.ai's **"Deep Code Analysis"** to detect redundant patterns and inefficient logic.

Step 3 Apply AI-Suggested Improvements

Refact.ai proposes

- **Extracting common logic into reusable functions.**
- **Optimizing database queries with AI-driven indexing suggestions.**
- **Refactoring large functions into modular components.**

Step 4 Validate Performance Improvements

After applying AI-powered refactoring, measure improvements in **code readability, execution speed, and maintainability**.

AI-powered refactoring with **Refact.ai** revolutionizes the way developers optimize legacy code. By **automating the identification of code smells, redundant logic, and inefficiencies**, Refact.ai significantly reduces manual effort while improving software maintainability.

THE END